Dinner Time

by Barbara L. Luciano
illustrated by Ginna Magee

Scott Foresman
is an imprint of

PEARSON

Glenview, Illinois • Boston, Massachusetts • Mesa, Arizona
Shoreview, Minnesota • Upper Saddle River, New Jersey

Every effort has been made to secure permission and provide appropriate credit for photographic material. The publisher deeply regrets any omission and pledges to correct errors called to its attention in subsequent editions.

Unless otherwise acknowledged, all photographs are the property of Pearson.

Photo locations denoted as follows: Top (T), Center (C), Bottom (B), Left (L), Right (R), Background (Bkgd)

Illustrations by Ginna Magee

Photograph 8 Corbis

ISBN 13: 978-0-328-39292-6
ISBN 10:   0-328-39292-8

1 2 3 4 5 6 7 8 9 10 V010 17 16 15 14 13 12 11 10 09 08

Two horses eat this dinner.

Four chicks eat this dinner.

One pig eats her dinner.

Mom looks at her watch.

It is five o'clock.

We are eating dinner too.

Animals on the Move

Read Together

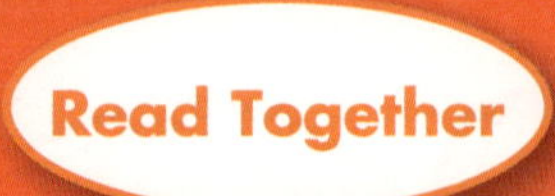

All the animals in this book eat. All the animals can move too. Animals have different ways to move. Some animals walk on feet. Some animals use fins to swim. Some animals even hop! What other ways can animals move?

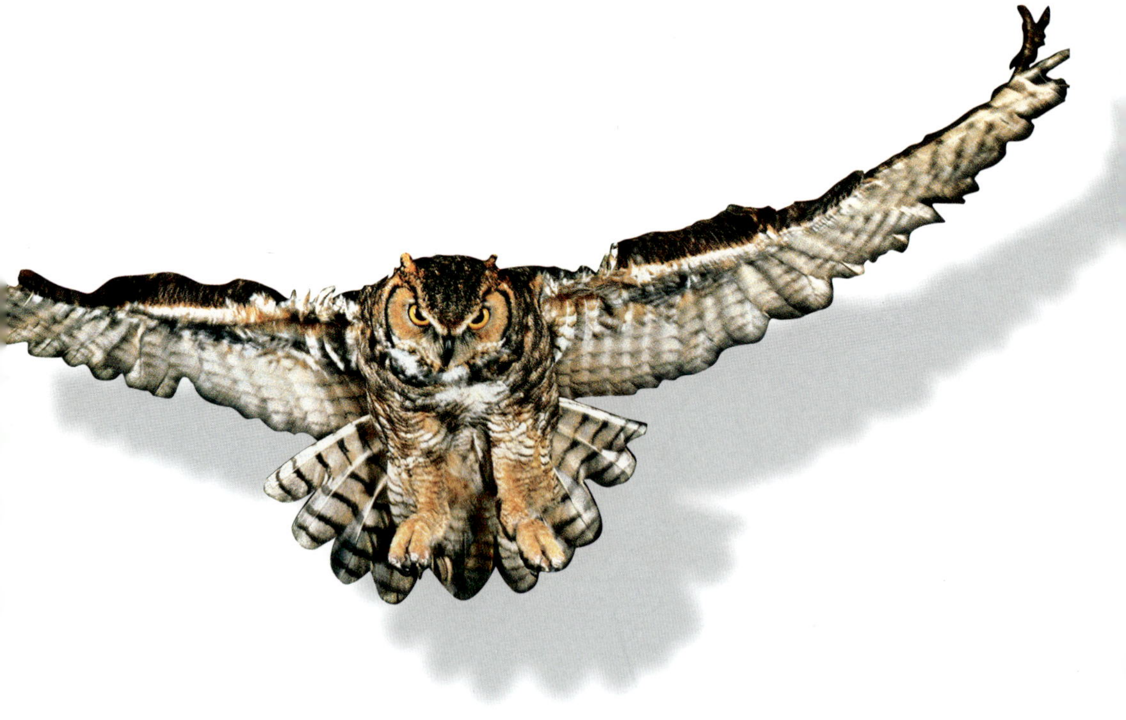